Let Her Run

J. Raymond

ISBN: 1522904670
ISBN-13: 978-1522904670

DEDICATION

This collection is only possible because of the success of Spades, my first modest, and unexpected attempt at writing a book. An individual's writing style should change, and evolve, over the course of a career. The words on these pages are not my best, but they are honest, and I will continue to grow as a writer.

Keep growing with me.

This book is dedicated to you.

*The numbered pieces with an asterisk next to them indicate an actual custom piece I was commissioned to write.

ACKNOWLEDGMENTS

Cover Artwork by Jessica Barros

i

Let Her Run

J. Raymond

1

She does not need the entire world,
only someone to take her
where she's never been before.
Love comes in different shapes, sizes
and landscapes,
with various skylines and heights
full of beautiful and terrifying sights.
Take her high enough to kiss the sun,
then
at night
watch her come down like rain.
Take her to those places
she no longer remembers pain.

I'm telling you,
if you go far enough,
everything changes.
Even you.

No,
she does not need the entire world.

You can't force her to fall, no matter the cost.
She just wants to run,
knowing you've never really loved
unless you've been lost.

2

Everything I saw in the world,
I saw in her.
And I don't just mean all the clichéd pretty things.
I mean the real,
raw,
and gritty things.

Often lost
and occasionally missing.
The world won't wait.
It cannot wait.
And it demands to be respected.
Watch how naturally it moves on,
with or without you.
It is as unstable
as it is contained.

Even the brightest stars eventually fall,
still full of more life than we could experience
in ten lifetimes,
a gentle shower
could lead to rough winds and torrential rains.

She was my butterfly effect,
and I craved her waves.
I guess what I'm trying to say
is that I was afraid,
and I just wanted to be a part of her world.

3

Falling in love, for her
came all too easily.
So she learned to love the world from its edges,
shadows,
and safe distances—
to stay the hell away from her feelings.

What a dangerous way to live—

seeing the beauty in everyone
and everything,
yet keeping it all
just out of arms reach.

We can't help but fall for women
like her.
Knowing they'll never be entirely ours,
but going half-crazy
just to be sure.

I respected the way she respected the things
that could take her breath away.

Anyway,
I didn't trust much in this world,
but I sure as hell trusted her.

And I suppose that was worth going mad over.

4

It wasn't that the world was out to get her.
She just made it harder on herself sometimes.
I guess that is one of the side effects
of having a heart that's always wide open.
She wasn't quite sure
if what she was letting in
or out
was right
or wrong.
But, my God,
she felt everything.

You have to understand that some wildflowers
carry both the pollen
and the poison.
Living with that much life and death
could grow tiresome.
Feeling too much
instead of growing numb.

I wasn't sure whether to run from her
or towards her.
So I ran with her.

And for the first time
in a long time,

I believed in something.

5

I feel sorry for those of you who tell yourself
to only feel love
because you'll never survive a woman like her.
She's not all prim,
proper
and made of daises.
Her curtsies come in the form of middle fingers
and spitfire.
And the way she would lose her fucking cool
always warmed my soul.

They say to love.
Just love.
Love everything.
Love will set you free,
free to pretend to love even more things…..

STOP.

Please don't hold
or choke a single thing back.
If you want to snap,
snap.
Don't paint a fake smile on your face to hide your fangs.
And can't we accept that some horses
can't be broken
and shouldn't be tamed?
Buck the system
and every last trend.
Are you listening?
You're not meant to be contained.

Passion
has love,
and a million other things too.
I'll welcome each of them,
if you just take me with you.

6

I don't know much about women,
but I do know this:
what was most important,
were that you held her interest
and kept her safe.
Ironic,
I suppose—
she was looking for the things she already possessed.

I've always respected the ones
unable to recognize their own strength.
You simply cannot stare at the sun.

Here was a girl who had the world by the throat
but could barely make it out of bed some mornings.
She would make it through,
albeit misguided,
and find that everything worth finding
was always out of the way.

She both adored
and avoided people.
She'd find herself in songs,
and art,
and seasons,
and stories.
And by the time you caught up,
you were so far off the beaten path,
you couldn't go back.
Or no longer wanted to.

It was then,
or there,
in the middle of nowhere,
that it all made sense -
    loving her would be an adventure.

7

The world was changing,
as was she.
You didn't have to like it,
but you'd best respect it.
Chances are,
when you go looking for her,
she won't be home anymore.
What an enticing way to live—

always going somewhere,
yet never setting plans in stone.

Sometimes
she wouldn't say anything at all,
she'd simply observe—
seeing the wonder in things naturally.

I watched her the same way.

When a balloon finds itself with no hand to hold it,
it does not sit and wait.
I'm not sure if I'll ever catch her,
but I promised myself
I'd watch her rise higher,
to see how far she would go.
She was nothing
if not completely alive
and totally free.

8

She still believed in love.
But if you asked her why,
she likely could not tell you.

You could see it though,
the wild in her eyes.
Seeing things
not as they could be,
but as if everything that made them ugly
might also make them beautifully misunderstood.

The most perfect things can't seem
to stay in one place for too long.
The moon shines in stages,
the tide must subside,
and eventually,
the sun will rise.

I guess love was a trust thing.
And if eyes were the windows to the soul,
hers were the only ones I cared to know.

She believed in love
because she believed in herself.

9

Somewhere between what she'd survived
and who she was becoming
was exactly where she was meant to be.
She was beginning to love the journey
and find comfort
in the quiet corners
of her wildest dreams.

They say people don't change.
Well,
she wasn't always this way.
Even if she did not change the entire world,
she would change her part of it.
And she would affect those she shared it with.

A butterfly
whose wings have been touched
can indeed still fly.
Whether something was meant to be
or meant to leave
no longer mattered as much.

She would soak up the sun,
kiss the breeze,
and she would fly

regardless.

10

It wasn't that she would shut down.
She just understood words weren't always needed
for her to find herself.
She had to leave the world behind at times.
Maybe the clearest reflection
can only be found
once you lose your sense of direction.
She tossed the maps
and pressed her ear to that Northern Star ever-present in her heart.
And really,
what was she leaving behind
besides a past
from which lessons had already been learned?

She carried her own seasons with her,
and you have to accept
that winter would always be one of them.
But so was spring.
She'd be back.
And I knew that everything this world needed
would come back to life
alongside her.

The world didn't revolve around her.
She revolved around it.
So let her run.

11

You thought she was lost,
and what fools we all are—
thinking a girl like her,
whose toes have tipped rock bottom before,
needed saving.
Really,
all she wanted was someone who would do
exactly what they said they would do.
She already knows how to do it alone;
only she no longer wants to.

Maybe I'm different,
or women like her are different
and I just get it.

I understand that being alone is easier
than being around people who don't understand you.
I recognize the way walls can close in by the inch.
And if she has a point to prove,
I just go ahead and accept it.

Easiest way to get a woman like her
to accomplish something?
Tell her she can't.

I guess I'll always respect anything with that much pride
and independence
rolled into one.
Something that beautiful
was never intended to be saved
by just anyone.

Perhaps it was her outstretched wings
or the flowers in her hair.
I can't help but fall for the free spirited
it seems.
The ones afraid of settling down
or settling at all.
She was a wanderer.
But only because her plans,
once written in stone,
turned to sand.
Washed away by the waves of change.

Girls like her
eventually learn to protect themselves
from themselves.
The people they are today
are not the people they were yesterday.
And gypsies like that are bound to have broken hearts.

That was the connection I felt.

We knew the higher you were brave enough to fly,
the further the fall.
She wasn't lost in love.
She was lost
and in love.
She didn't know where the hell she was heading
and never really seemed to care.

I only wanted to make sure she never got there.

13

When it comes to loving her,
you had better assert yourself.
Bring everything you have—

your razor wit
and sharp intellect.
She's not meant for the gun-shy or timid.

Truth is,
she's not even looking for love.
She knows it can't be pinpointed,
baited,
or caged.
True love cannot be captured
because it could never escape.

She's a wild heart
with a soul free flowing—
still that little girl holding on too tight,
but who'd learned to swing her feet.

Can't you see the stars more clearly
when standing in places furthest off the beaten path?
Is the ocean not deeper
the further out you head from shore?

Even where it's dark,
there is both beauty
and an abundance of life.
Loving her
was worth every risk
you were brave enough to take,

and most especially
the ones you were too afraid to.

Maybe she is out of control.
It's possible her past had made her that way.
If you ask me,
she simply hadn't yet decided
who she wanted to be.
Always more than what met the eyes,
she was never meant to keep her feet on the ground,
and her ink told stories of her journey.
Her memories charted the course,
and her dreams told truths
that her mind wouldn't believe
but which her heart understood -
it knew.

It was that whisper at night
reminding her she was meant to be elsewhere.
I just wanted to be there
with her.
To show her shorelines
and sunsets
and midnight fires.
To hear her tell stories
after too many drinks
and not have a clue what tomorrow would bring -

and to not give a damn about it.

Maybe she was out of control.
Maybe death,
to her,
was anything predictable.
And she knew what most of us forget:
life was too short
to wake up for
or fall in love with
anything that felt ordinary.

15

She is only hard to understand
to those who sound like everyone else,
and she will always feel cold
to those who do not warm her soul.
She's not bitter,
her words just aren't sugarcoated.

A rainbow
birthed from hurricanes.
The most valuable things
need not always shine.

When she glances at herself in the mirror,
trust that it's not a matter of vanity.
It's to make sure her smile
still points to the stars.

I guess what I'm trying to say
is that I still know all that glitters
isn't gold.
But everything that doesn't
isn't dull.

16

She was happy
but in a genuinely raw way.
The kind of happiness that grows from the muck.
The kind that makes her impossible
to handle for anyone spineless.
She has questions which need answering.
She wants to know everything.
Your history,
your nightmares,
every city you've visited.

So we talked.
And she listened.
Christ,
I showed her my soul
like she was saving me.
When really,
she was traveling someplace new
through me.

She was terrified of the things she should love
and loved the things which should've terrified her.
We spoke of the same pains.
Who hurts you more than those closest?

Yes,
she was twisted
and confused
and not well rested.

But she listened
like time didn't matter.
And for once
everything stood still.
Everything except her heart.

That would always be wild

in a genuinely raw way.

17

To hell with your opinions of her.
To hell with whatever you thought
made her less than everything.
She did exactly what she wanted to do
and owned every last misstep and flaw.
Do you really believe there is anything you can say
that is worse than what she has actually lived through?

The same thread on which she tenuously hung,
she used to sew herself back up with.
And had learned not to keep company
with those wielding knives.
She'd rather have a small circle
than an empty one.
Lines were crossed,
and her heart was now dead set on the horizon.
Anything less than what she deserved
fell behind.

Understand something:
she was never drowning.
The day that some people in her world
became an anchor
was the day she learned to swim.

18

You and I,
we've had our moments.
Moments that altered our outlook
and made us change directions.
And while the world was offering up its condolences
and advice,
I knew it was moot.
We did not need guidance.
The lessons were ours to learn,
and there wasn't a damn thing I could do
or say
to make these bruises fade.
But we were not the same.
She wanted to wear them proudly.
She earned them after all.
And every last shot that life fired on her,
she absorbed.

Do not pity,
coddle,
or patronize her.
She will not allow it.
The trivial things didn't worry her anymore.
Thunder doesn't whisper through the rain.
A tidal wave takes whatever it wants.
Only fools fight strong winds.

She didn't know exactly where she'd end up,
but she knew how to set the sails in her favor.
And she was a force
to be reckoned
and
to be wrecked with.

19

Just because she is not meant to be alone
does not mean she is meant for everyone.
I asked her once,
"What are you really looking for?"
She didn't know.
She didn't even care to know.
And I didn't seem to mind that about her.

Some women come with agendas:
Get a degree,
meet dream man,
get married,
have a family,
and die happily ever after.

The types I'm drawn to,
have had weekend benders
and come with too much baggage.
They relate more to Alice
than any Princess.
They've gone mad.

Tell me about your heartbreaks and mistakes.
We'll swap horror stories
over eighty proofs.
Some people have plans,
others have problems.
And it's amidst the darkness,
the grime and shit,

that everything I find perfect in a woman exists.
Don't you dare feign perfection
or talk proper near me.

I want your past, your lessons, your tragedies.
Some people want nothing but the best for you,
but I believe it's the hells and its fires
that forged you.

Wherever we are going
is because of where we've been.
Be proud of us.

You might not recognize her anymore.
Things are different now.
She is beginning to make sense
of who she's becoming.
Sure,
it took some time to get here,
and maybe she had taken a few ill-advised turns.
But the long way
isn't always the wrong way.

Her route,
her rules.

Everything which made her beautiful
made her slightly unusual too.
She would challenge you,
sweet-lipped,
but with a look which was deliberate.
A gaze that carried weight
and always meant something significant.

Some things were never meant to be singular.
And when they change,
it's because they have to.
Not to fit in
or stand out,
but to survive.
You might not have a say in that
or even be able to make much sense of her,
but she gets it.
She understands that she really can be
whoever she wants to be
so long as she stays herself.

She felt for things,

people,
and each moment
wholeheartedly.

Some carry so much conviction
and life within
that they are never truly alone.
You will never take that from her.

21

My hope is that we dance,
wild and uninhibited,
and that we laugh until our eyes tear.

But
if you're not one of the ones on the dance floor,
I hope you're the one pouring the drinks.
And if you're not the one pouring,
I hope you're the one drinking
to something
or someone.
I hope you're living your own life
and doing things you once thought impossible.
I hope you break all the way down,
toss away that last bit or armor,
lay your gun down at your feet,
and come to me with flaws in hand.

I hope you never become a sheep
and that you're still living for the thrill.
I hope you never bite your tongue,
and always let your imagination run rampant.
And while you're running off the edge,
I hope you pick a few flowers to share
with those who matter most.
And for God's sake,
I hope you go far
while still remembering to dance wildly.

And if you forget,
I hope the person who kisses you on your forehead each night
is me.
And in the morning
when I ask,
"Are you awake?"
I hope you can answer honestly.

22

She was godless at times,
yet always full of faith.
And if she never counted millions,
she would still be rich.

Even if she never traveled the world,
she would make memories worth revisiting.

Please don't assume that because she has yet to find the right one,
she, herself, isn't exactly that.
And if you find her with nothing,
she will still be fulfilled.
Her heart will be heavy now and again
and she will always be flawed to her core.

Love lives in the eye of the storm.
Beauty
in an imperfect smile.
And that is it -
Her heart and mind were ablaze,
and that would never be safe for some.

Know this:
what you value owns you.

And even if she gave you her body,
the rest would need to be earned.

No need to weigh heartaches or mistakes.
If you search for yourself in song
or story,
you are already unlike the rest of them.
Kink your veins, I say.
A black sheep
with armored wool -
you're not always meant for this world,
but goddamn it,
life,
it's about time you fell into place.
Have we not sacrificed enough already?
It's time to settle up.

Give us bottomless love,
wounds which heal themselves,
and dreams that actually go as planned.

We're such fools for hope.
And even when we should have none left
we hope still.

It's like this:
I want to know you,
the parts of you this world keeps trying to extinguish.
But you burn.
Burn this motherfucker down.
I want to see it,
and I know,
I just know,
there's a fire in you ready to be set free.

That's the thing about people who lose it all—

to them,
everything matters.

24

I'm begging you -
find the loves of your life.
The things you are made for
which are made for you.
There's nothing for you in the gray area,
no heart in transition
death is in the in-between.

When you need to rest,
rest.
Just understand that some will not wait for you.
A few will.
And fewer still
are the ones who will wait *with* you

So rest.
Then run.
Run in lockstep
alongside them.
Love harder.
Trust again.
Cut ties to anything or anyone
holding you back -
your past,
your mistakes,
missteps, and heartbreaks.

I don't believe this world has seen your best just yet.

It's about time you carve your name in it.

25

What a fallacy it is to think putting pressure on her
would do anything other than force her to grow.

If the ocean
crashing into mountainsides
eventually breaks it down,
then she would always be the waves.
Aggressive some days
and calm on others.
But always present
and ever constant.

She had been through her own hells
and was made stronger by its fires.
Being forged from a few failures
yields a different type of strength—

the type which reminds you
you can survive anything
and are smart enough
to not make the same mistakes twice.
She was nothing,
if not a force.
Whether or not she knows that
or feels that,
would still hold true
every day.

The further out you go from shore,
the deeper it is to the ocean floor.
Even where there was pressure
there was life,
and that's all she would ever need
in order to grow.

26

She was the type of girl who would always
have books strewn about,
clothes on her floor,
and a few dishes not yet put away.
Her life was just like that.
She had everything she needed,
just not always organized.
Even still,
she would eventually find everything
she was looking for.

Maybe not everything needed a place,
and maybe not everyone had found theirs quite yet either.
And while the world was steadily chasing her down
to find that place,
I just loved the way she kept going.

She went in all different directions,
and I swear
if I had the guts,
I would do the same.
Maybe her life was unkempt,
and maybe it wasn't always orderly,
but she was living it exactly her way.

And anything that did not make her feel alive
would have to find its place
in someone else's world.

Don't come to me with your favorite color
and your astrology sign.
No,
tell me instead about the things which keep you
up at night
and the knives still in your back.
Tell me about the dreams you gave up on
and your drug of choice.
I'm not going to read in-between the lines
you've already written with bloody ink.
Everything you have
you have
because of what you've been through.

When you are staring in the mirror,
tell me what you've seen.
I've been off track so often
that I don't even pretend to know where I'm heading.
I only know I won't be going on every adventure alone.
If you're accompanying me,
I need to know that you're not afraid
of what we might find around every corner.

So tell me about the wrong turns you've made
which led you to who you are today.

Show me the parts of you
that others don't see,
and I'll show you why you should never hide
from the world you deserve.

28

I wish I could tell you that she was the bravest person
you would ever meet,
that she learned her lessons,
she knew exactly what she wanted
and had finally found her way.

I wish I could tell you that she was the calm before the storm
and not the storm itself.
Maybe her skin wasn't as thick as you thought
after being rubbed raw by life,
and that she still takes everything at face value.
But that is not her – not anymore.

She found beauty and romance in things
most others overlooked.
Like airports
and the way an old record player cracks and pops.
She found it in the ink she earned
and the way the stars seemed brighter
on the darkest nights.

I wish I could tell you that she was the bravest person
you'd ever meet,
but
if you met her
you would never need me to.

I'd understand if you fell for her.
I wouldn't blame you for seeing some of the same things
that I see.
But to get her to reciprocate,
you'll need to go deeper.
Dig,
and reach her other levels.

Understand that for everything she isn't,
there's plenty she already is.
She stopped trying to be perfect long ago.

Watch her.

I mean it.

Just watch the way she gets back up
and manages to make bandages beautiful.
When you've loved things with as much force as she has,
you lose some of yourself along the way.

Thank her for that.

Don't you see more than her surface?
And that it's not the exterior that's gold?
Even a blind fool can fall for what she was born with.
But she'll only give herself
to the one who falls
for what she's earned.

So if you have to ask what it is I see in her,
just know it's things you never will.

30

I'm not sorry if she wasn't what you expected.
Maybe that was your first mistake—
expecting.
And the next was likely expecting her
to be like someone you've met before.

She'll never be just one thing.
Goddamn it,
give her a good night sleep
and a flint to dream upon,
and I swear she'll become the sun.

But even the sun must set
to rise.
And when it's too dark for her to reach her destiny,
even from the tips of her toes,
will you lift her?
If not,
leave her,
spare her,
save her.
But if you're in it for something bigger
and brighter
than yourself,
I hope you fight.

Because even though she never imagined herself here,
she's right here entirely.
And she still imagines.

I've never been into the ones with no depth.
Who can't get themselves to see the appeal
in sin
or don't have a little evil in their eyes.
I prefer the unpolished gem—
far from perfect,
yet still worth it.

I need to know that you have survived a few long drops
and that you know how to speak directly to my demons.
It should require some effort to hold her close,
don't you think?
Give me the girl with her guard up
because she knows that when she falls,
she falls all the way down.
The ones who've never been the square peg
to the world's rabbit hole.
And who've learned their way around
the darkest parts of their own souls.

I love that you wear bruises like passport stamps,
and I want us to be an adventure.
I'm starting to understand that every path
to every person
is unique.
I just want to run with someone brave enough
to not need a path at all.

32

It was harder now that she had learned not to chase after
dead ends and dull people.
But there would always be something inside her
that brought her to the absolute edge.
She couldn't help but get too close,
lean over,
and peer down.
And it was the way she looked,
smiling off the ledge,
that summed up everything I found beautiful.

Because down there
were a few things she learned she could live without.
They were once parts of her,
parts that mattered immensely.
Broken dreams,
severed heartstrings,
lost loves,
childhood memories,
and who she once believed she was.

And still,
she leaned over
and she always smiled.

You should know
she's not lacking.
Those places where parts of her were missing
were simply spaces for wings.
If angels have to die
to come back to life,
then she would never have a fear of falling
once she learned she could fly.

33

A chance would always be
all she'd ever need.
And really,
what are we
other than the remains of our hopes and dreams?

She's an antique
which,
after all this time,
still shines underneath.
Not everyone has an eye for that sort of thing though.

I hope you know that the most painfully beautiful things
never fight for our attention.
The ocean never boasts.
The moon isn't always full.
And that field of flowers will return
just to remind us all that it never actually left.

And maybe I'm a romantic,
or maybe I finally learned
to let the ocean pull me in,
to slow down and appreciate the moon for once,
and to stop plucking flowers.

A chance would always be all she'd ever need.
And that would always be the one thing
she should never
and would never
have to ask me for.

34

You want empathy from a world
that will most likely never understand you.
From your fingerprints
straight through to your marrow,
you're wildly different.
You're not at all what we see,
and if ever there was something to love about you,
it would be that.

When the world hands you its rulebook,
your eyes and heart wander.
From the outside
looking in,
you're stunning.
But from the inside
looking out,
we both know it's not always that way.

You're a rogue wave at times
and the furthest thing from honey.
A complex mess of a girl
with a knotted heart—
determined
not to be understood,
but to understand.

They'll speak as if they know your journey
better than you do.
They'll judge your smile,
your tears,
and everything in-between
as if everyone deserves your best.
They don't.
You do.

35

If I had just one more chance,
just one more day,
I'd spend it lying next to you.
And it's not a sexual thing,
though there'd be plenty of that.
It's about getting as much honesty out of each minute
that remains.

We've both spent too much time
trying to be something we aren't
for someone else.
Let's just be us,
for us.
That has to be enough.

No masks.
No games.
No apologies.
No words.

Just a couple shells in these sheets,
hands and legs locked.
I know you're strong,
don't be.
I know you're brave,
there's no need.
I've been dying this entire time,
but this bottle won't be the death of me.
Let this moment overflow my lungs with something stronger.

Do you see what you've done?
If I could have one more chance,
I'd kill myself convincing you that
you
are
everything.
And anyone who makes you feel like less
is nothing at all.

Nothing is an accident,
not even her shortfalls.
So she'd never be the type to leave her heart on the shelf
for too long.
And while we're all trying to be superheroes,
she already knows the real weight behind
living up to your word.
Whoever it is that you want her to believe you are,
be that
every day.

It's not that she is impossible,
she simply has her mind set
on where her heart is set
this time around.
Too many before you committed themselves
to a purpose
or a place
instead of the person.
And I'd tell you that's where you went wrong with her,
except nothing is an accident.

So she learned to love how the day would begin
without knowing how it might end.
It's not about being perfect.
It's about being unstoppable,
the strongest things all seem to be that way.
And too many before you
committed themselves to the wrong things.

She is going to take some time.
It just wouldn't feel like it was being taken from you.
More like you were making room for her.

Girls like her were always standing behind velvet curtains,
and if you wanted to know the real them,
you'd best have patience.
Anything worth a damn demands time
and a little effort.
The problem with a lot of people these days
is they can't wait for the things worth waiting for.

Trading substance for things superficial
and a future
for a few heartbeats they'll never really feel.

So when I hold her hands,
she would recognize the backs of them.
And I'll learn about the dirt under her nails,
the lines and every lesson in her palms,
the map of her fingerprints,
and truly
feel her grip.

I'll finally hear her real voice
and know the whole truth,
her oddities
and intricacies.
And I swear
if you can't understand why that is worth waiting for
then I hope you can understand why she won't be there
when you come back looking for her.

38

You're telling me that what's right is right
and what's wrong
is wrong.
As if her life was in black and white.
What about the girls who make wrong feel right
and push boundaries,
who bite their lips
and ball their fists?
Some just have good intentions
bad judgment,
and can admit to making love to a few mistakes.

See,
I believe she was made in the unknown,
in the gray fog of transition
and second guessing.
And if you'd wait for the weather to worsen,
you'd see that the way she dances in the rain
is anything but choreographed.
It's wildest
during its worst,
but she dances nonetheless.

She wasn't right.
She wasn't wrong.
She was always herself,
which was different
and more than enough.

The truth is
she doesn't need much.
Least of all, were things she could get herself.
So here's to the little things which add up to everything.

You want to make her dreams come true
and all she needs is someone with whom to rest gently
and wake up alongside slowly.
Someone with words set in stone
and a mind wide open.

Show her what chivalry looks like,
what attention sounds like,
and what passion feels like.
It's not that she has lesser expectations,
she just knows what actually matters now.
Different traits carry different weights.

I know we're not always good at these things,
but that's not a good enough excuse anymore.
She deserves your best,
and so do you.
Look her in the eyes
and tell her
"You matter to me more than you know.
I don't want any of this without you,
and,
outside of us,
I don't need much either."

And maybe,
in that moment,
you'll see her believe in something other than herself again.

40

I'm telling you
she does not belong.
Not to one person,
not to one place,
not to one set of ideals.
Her mind changed her heart,
which changed her mind over again.
She was nothing
if not completely free.

Maybe we're just afraid of anyone constantly searching.
Anything that didn't clip her wings
or make her feel caged
was exactly where she was meant to be.
You've got to respect the things unafraid of going off path.
And she would always be the type
to lose herself
trying to find her own ways.

I suppose the river doesn't compete with the earth,
it carves its own path.
It doesn't brag,
or boast,
or beat its chest.
It just flows.
And the moon doesn't try to outshine the stars.
It just glows.
The flowers
amidst the trees
which radiate and create life,
they only grow.

She wasn't free because she knew where she was going.
She was free because she didn't need to know.

41

Show some respect
for anyone willing to undress themselves
in front of you.
A woman with her heart stark naked
and soul exposed.

Love her in the middle of each indecency,
and begin to accept that she is not concerned
with your acceptance.

Watch for the ones who grab the world
by its throat,
yet also know when to reach for its hand.
Applaud the ones who have been broken down
by life,
yet somehow still manage to stand confidently
in the face of it all.

Give me the ones full of flaws,
over anyone with masked facades.
I want your real character in the raw,

and I understand that everyone wants what they can't have
until they have it.

But I want the things I can have
because everyone else cannot,
should not,
and never truly deserved them.

42

You can never be too certain
about some.
I suppose that's what keeps us coming back.

She was esoteric,
entirely awake,
and made up of many of the traits
we can't seem to get enough of.
Imperfect, incomplete,
yet still more than most.

And if her silence did not speak volumes,
her outlook most surely would……

Her favorite color – the rain
Her favorite things – came from a previous era,
    and seemed to be made for her especially.
    Antique, vintage, something with a history.

She was like every word I had yet to learn the meaning of,
but still knew existed somewhere,
that had its place.
She was complex,
and each of her pieces
made her that much more of a rarity.

I've always gone into it all believing
I needed to figure them out,
I needed to better understand them.

Perhaps she is a mystery
never intended to be solved,

and I hope she knows that should we make it to the end
we can keep going
beyond everything we know to be true.

43

Every time.
Every single time,
   she went too far
   too hard.

I wonder if she knew how rarely anything ever
works out,
and how it's never as planned.
Not that it would have mattered.

It's as if she only knows how to feel
wholeheartedly,
to sing from the tops of her lungs,
and hurt
down to her marrow.

Life, for her,
was never enough without passion,
there was never a toeing of the line.

I loved the way she went up in flames,
and down
just the same.
You could not take your eyes off of her,
and sometimes
all that is needed to stand out
is to stand back up.

We pay close attention to those bruised deepest,
who are still brave enough to try taming the beast.
She goes too far,
   too hard

because anything less
feels like nothing at all.
And we all should be so lucky to feel what happens
when the things liable to ruin us

have the breath ripped from their own lips willingly.

What fools we are
for fearing the beast

more so than the one
with enough love and conviction
to tame it.

44

She is the type of girl who can have anybody,
yet cannot be had.

Like a lock with a missing key,
a story incomplete.

And she left her impression on you -
like lipstick on a napkin
or in a song you hear years later
and still somehow know all the words to.

Go for the girl who has been around,
who has seen the way the world crumbles
but also knows how to piece it back together.

She is not the easiest route,
nor the calmest waters.
She's a hailstorm in an open field.
A back alley tsunami.
A mirage,
an uncut diamond,
the perfect mistake

and a million other impossibilities.

Understand that rarity does not exist under every stone,
or around every corner.
She has to be selective -
   not from a level of superiority.
It's a self-worth thing,

and passion should be suffocating,
ecstasy
that is overwhelming.

So think twice,
but move swiftly,
kiss deeply

and do not back down.

She cannot be had,
but she can be proven right -
   or wrong.

That part is up to you.

45

We will come around
eventually.
But for now,
pull her in closer
knowing a heart is only a bomb,
and her lips
the trigger.

The same thing which will rescue you
might make you take cover.
Yet we run to it.
We dress it up with words as soft as butterfly wings
and decorated in lace.

It's a vile thing should it end.

A pinless grenade held between two hands.

It's not that you shouldn't trust her,
it's that you're afraid to die for her.
But loving without risk
isn't loving at all.
And living too far from the edge
never comes with a view.

Get closer to her,
carefully,
it's a long drop down
and it happens in an instant.

The climb back up may take a lifetime,
but love is simply two people meant to hurt perfectly
together.
Let it.
Die, smiling
alongside her.

46

I remember every last thing I know I should forget.
Certain songs cannot be unheard,
the strongest feelings
never go unfelt.

I am no longer who I once was,
and she is not at all who she seems.
She is made from what she has seen,
and as a result of what she's survived.

I loved everything most others wanted her to hide,
and if I had to choose -
I would opt for her laughing
and her at her most natural state,

over anything else in this world.

There is this shyness to her,
and I am not sure if it has always been a part of her,
or if someone made her that way

but I do find that the quietest ones
always have the most to say,
the wildest stories,

and the deepest seeded pains.

Though soft,
she could cut her way through you.
We seem to have a difficult time understanding
the ones most fragile, I find.
In truth,
it's the ones untested, unbroken
who aren't worth the climb.

She,
like most everything beautifully imperfect,

had missing pieces you both could learn to look through.

Like I said,
some things cannot be unseen, or unfelt.
I am only trying to see it all,
remember every fine detail,

And never overlook the very best of her.

47

After all this time
I am drawn most to an individual's perspective
and imagination.
The ones who know what really matters to themselves.

Do you not see so much life growing beneath your feet?

I'm a fool for looking for love in everything,
maybe,
but I have been through enough to know how crippling
life can be.
So sing with me,
let us dance with reckless abandon.
Unfurl your fists,
and take my hand.

Let me tell you a story of a girl
who was brave enough to give up on a few dreams
so that she, herself,
may come true.

Someone who has also been through enough,
seen and felt enough
to know that not everything was meant to reach her heart.

I wonder if you will ever see yourself
as I see you tonight.
You do deserve to feel love with every one of your senses.

I am broken down,
you are broken down,
we have both removed all of the excuses
and shed ourselves of the lies.

At the end of it all,
when we weren't enough for ourselves,

we will always be enough for someone else.

So tell me again what it is that you see,
and who you imagine yourself to be.

She has gone wayward,
abandoning plans on promised roads leading nowhere.
Life can go awry,
and she could go astray at times,
but there seems to be only one way to learn most lessons.

You go through fire,
to be forged by it,
and I never fault her for being hardened in ways.
I do not blame her.

A barb-wired heart
protecting the softness she once was.

If you are close enough to touch her,
you are close enough to respect her.
Steel grows slowly,
and though force will make it bend,
it remains strong.
Strong enough for two.

It is an oddity of life
we still attempt to make sense of:
  how someone with such an ugly past
  still manages to turn themselves into art.
They get eaten up by the vile,
yet become a flower with deeper roots.

Selfish temptation makes us want to pluck them
from the ground they grew themselves from,
while all along
the answer has been to simply breathe in the same air as her,
allow her to outshine the others,
and know
through it all

she will continue to grow.

49

There was a time she had it mostly figured out.
There was a time when answers seemed clearer,
each step more calculated,
the future mapped out,
important dates recorded and circled.

Life was not easy, but it made sense to her.

The world has a habit of making examples
out of girls like her.
Powerful, to me,
are never the ones with the trophies and bright smiles,

but the ones who have been left for dead
yet come up swinging.
The girl with the bloody lip
still walking steadfast in one direction:
forward.

Do not show me pictures of the girl who has gotten
everything she has ever asked for.
Take me to the girl with dirt under her nails
from digging her own graves.
Who has repeated the same mistakes,
is not afraid of regrets,
who now understands that you cannot design a life.

Life is unpredictable -
   so she learned to laugh more often and easily.

Life is hard -
   so she learned when to be soft.

Life is beautiful -
   so she learned where to look.

Life is short -
   so she learned to make it significant.

Life is a bitch -
   so she became a better one.

50

Know this of the girl:

she speaks in waves
and still smiles with little reason.
She wishes upon stars she does not know the names of,
and prays to Gods who are not always listening.

Still,
with filament heartstrings
she holds on tightly to fractured dreams.

We need more like her......

ones who trust actions above all else,
but still believe in the unseen.
Cutting through shade and shadow,
and watch the way she shines through it all.

Her hands carry you past abandoned buildings,
through city streets and old, run-down theaters.
You let her, and you watch her as if everything you're seeing
and feeling
will begin to make sense soon.
You watch her
because you simply cannot stop yourself from doing so.

I say to give her all you have,
only because she has lost it all before.
If you have spirit to spare

give it to the girl able to make miracles of it.

51

We want what we want.
The reasons need not always add up.
When we touch what feels like fire,
it does bring us to life

before burning us to the ground.

And we want to live.
My God,
we want to feel alive again
if only for a moment.

Do not ask her why she does what she does.
Do not question how she comes back to life.

Throw yourself to the wind
and watch the way you learn to fly.
Do not worry about where you might land, love,

you will not be there for long.

You are only just now beginning,
and there is a world out there ready for you.
So much still left to see,
and breathe,
and feel,
and the very last thing you should be right now
is afraid......

but feel that as well.

Because we want what we want.
So breathe it in,
and feel what continues to set your soul on fire.

Remember all of those times you thought you were ruined?
You weren't there for long either.

Go slay everything.

Once more for the resilient.
A tip of the cap to those with both balance
and a backbone.
The ones believing in too lofty of dreams
get their flames snuffed out awfully early
these days.
We crush out and flick away lovers
like cigarette butts.
Used up bodies with nothing but a little filter left.

And we seem to forget that love is still the only feeling
which can both chill us to the bone,
as well as warm our entire soul
at the same time.

So salute the steadfast.
Make way for the broken hearted
starting from scratch,
  again.
Believe in the elusive.
Get back up,
and jump head first into the fire.

We see you looking us in the eyes
wondering if we understand what you've survived.
And I cannot speak for everyone,
but I do…
I've been there too.

I am no longer sure where we will be
this time
tomorrow,
I am not sure if we will make it,
but I promise to not watch you waste away
waiting for something that's never going to arrive.

Just because I may not be the one for you,
does not mean that I will be the one against you.

53

When you find her
you will not know what to make of her.
She is not the fairest,
nor the most assertive.
She is not the gentle breeze,
    or the quiet night.
She is not a soft whisper,
    or calm waters.

Listen now, because this part is crucial –
she will never be any of those things.
And for that reason alone,
I beg you to leave her be.

When you find her
you will not know what to make of her.
You will try to change her,
and that too
is the worst thing you could do to a free spirit.

To find the girl still evolving,
and to alter that -
to manipulate or stunt her in any way,
really is one of the biggest mistakes we can make.

Give her room to stretch,
some space to breathe.
She is only now understanding some of who she is –

that there are times she will be more whiskey
than water,
be filled with more questions
than answers,
and feel more past
than present.

When you find her
remind her that only the flawed are flawless,

and the world will not always be able to make sense of the ones
with no fear of flying,

or falling.

54

I am not suggesting that the woman
was afraid of life -
only that she walked through it
more carefully now,
with a greater awareness than before.

Time has a way of becoming most valuable
only after someone steals enough of it.
The seconds, minutes, hours
all gone for good.
An exchange for the moments and memories
she now carries with her still.

Who you see now
is not the same person you first met.
You tread through seasons
dragging monsters and enough history
behind you,
and you are no longer the same person
once on the other side of it all.

You shed yourself of what weighs you down
eventually.

So,
wander this world alongside her,
but do so while filling
each second with excitement
each minute with peace
each hour with passion
every year with adventure

and her life with value.

Hold tight to the notion that if she is giving you
some of her time
she is giving you
some of her life.

55

The trees bend,
remain bent,
but refuse to break.
Shifting winds whip through her hair,
and she pauses to decide how much of herself
she should allow it to take.
Close your eyes,
sweet girl,
and smile in the face of all things threatening.
Rest easy -
knowing you are unlike the others,
knowing there is a moral to your story.

I understand the need for answers.
I understand the hope for closure.
But you will get neither.
You are not here to make sense of the scars,
but to accept that they are intended to play a part
in exactly who you are.

Do not feel sorry for yourself,
for feeling everything from the inside out.
Do not feel sorry
for having to turn your back on a few
you still see clearly.
Do not apologize for moving on
and leaving some of this world behind.

Bend, but do not break.
Set free the pieces of yourself no longer needed.
We are all growing and dying
in ways,
and you just seem to do that a little more wildly
some days.

Not everything needs to be understood
to be appreciated.

56

Where to next?
What do you suppose lives out there,
just beyond the bend?

The weather is changing again,
did you notice?

I feel it most in the wind -
a lightness,
carrying something mysterious
and life-altering
this way.

Something serene,
Something reminding me of why you,
refusing to turn back,
refusing to surrender
was not easy,
but undoubtedly worth it.

Yes,
there is certainly something up ahead,
I can nearly see it,
just there

around the bend.

It is so much more than anything you expected,
or experienced thus far.
It feels like everything you deserve,
and so much less of what you never did.
I cannot wait to see what it makes of you.

Are you ready now?

57

A lot like coffee in bed,
like hearing that song you once loved
  but had forgotten about.
Like the beach after midnight,
like the perfect morning,
like the open roads,
like a familiar face after far too long apart.
Like hands which fit perfectly
in yours,
arms that welcome you home,
a smile
meant for you alone.

A lot like an afternoon shower
with every single window opened wide.
Like acoustics around a campfire,
like the harmonica
like the trees
like the faces lit from the fire
like the laughter turned amber
like all that really matters is this moment.

Like every insignificant
overlooked
underappreciated
taken for granted
misunderstood
thing
rolled into one.
Rolled into everything.

Like you.

I will not label you all things delicate.
I will not look for the gentlest comparisons,
the softest analogies
in some attempt to make you feel better about yourself.

Do you believe yourself to be a dandelion?
Since when did you become the ocean,
the moon,
a summer night,
or the fallen star?

That is not what you will get from me.
You've been through the thicket,
have you not?
And surely you must know
there will be more heartbreak along the way.
The journey is not over yet,
it does not end here,
and you are too bold to be a rainbow.

I trust who you honestly are, far too much,
to label you as some intangible hyperbole.
You are not always something this world will find pretty.

The most difficult part of it all, for some,
is learning how to live comfortably in their own skin.
To wake up on purpose,
with reason,
and continue to allow yourself to feel all that this life
has to offer.
The delicateness,
and also the ruthlessness.

You are not a sunflower,
or the sunshine,

or the sunrise,
or the sunlight,
you are you……
just as bright,
just as significant,
just as necessary.

59*

Sometime, the sparrow miscalculates
the butterfly grows its wings
and the tidal wave can be born.
Sometimes, the exact song needed
plays at the exact right time
and everything is just right again.
Sometimes, the wasp does not sting.
Sometimes, that field of wildflowers turn into weeds,
and sometimes,
it comes back heavy with new life.
Sometimes, the wrong turns
help us lose our ways.
Sometimes, the coffee is how we take it,
and sometimes,
the stray cat finds the door with milk beneath it.

Sometimes, the preacher gets it right.
Sometimes, the evilest eyes
so most clearly at night.
Sometimes, it takes only a kiss, one kiss,
and sometimes,
the backs of two hands brushing against each other
for the first time
is all it takes.

Sometimes, the paycheck is enough for food
or a plane ticket.
Sometimes, we chose the plane ticket.
Sometimes, she is haphazard,
and sometimes,

it isn't so easy to do the right thing.
Sometimes, she doesn't.
Sometimes, she is not the eye of the storm,
but the storm itself.
Sometimes, she has nothing left,
and sometimes,
she overflows with new life,
but always,
she endures.

60*

She was unlike the others.
Not simply in the physical sense,
   though stunning,
more in an enigmatic way.
As if there were secrets about herself
she knew, that we never would.
Secrets which made it so she walked this world
fearing very little.

At the core of it all,
once you reach the heart of the matter,
you either survive
or you die.
Even if in parts,
we take what has been spared
and leave the rest of us behind.

She was unlike the others.
Not simply in the physical sense,
though she was steadfast,
stubborn to some,
but more so because she was unstoppable.
As if she knew there was no turning back now.
That once you make it through the impossible,
once you bring yourself back to life,
only then
do you truly know what you are capable of.

Even if she was hardened,
what she was now, most of all,
was alive,
full of feeling,
made from things which breathe deeply
beat steadily
evolve
and change like the seasons themselves.

She was unlike the others.
Not simply because she was immoveable
when it mattered most,
but because she found her significance again.
And if not one single thing held power over her anymore,

then what else could she do,
other than change the world
herself?

61*

"*It was not supposed to be like this…*"
she said.

"*No? What was it supposed to be like then?*"

"*Lighter. More carefree. I'm not afraid of whatever else
might cross my path, I just know that some of it is going
to hurt much more than I'd like.
I'm not ashamed of who I am,
I'm proud of everything I have overcome,
I would just like some rest already.
I want to look love square in the eyes,
and really believe in it again.
I want to wake up with purpose,
and fall asleep knowing that I made at least some amount
of impact.
There are too many things I have yet to see
with my own eyes,
and I know the world is full of beauty and mystery,
but I haven't held enough of it myself
to actually expect any of it.
I hardly know what to do with it
when I do have it.
I cannot seem to get myself to trust the things
that have hurt me in the past,
yet I still feel like I might not survive for very long
without them.*"

"*Well, you will survive just fine.
And you will also not have to wait one single second longer
than is absolutely necessary.
Not everyone is built like you,
but everything that moves you deeply
is certainly built for you.
And THAT is exactly how it's supposed to be……*"

62*

And now,
even if she could straighten out her curves,
or make alterations,
she wouldn't.
Her eyes were brown, and that was that.
Her smile was genuine.
Her laugh was easy.
Her passion, her own.

The imperfections
along with all of the things she once kept hidden,
now were parts of something she found beautiful,
sexy even.
We look at one another
and learn how to focus in on faults.
We see each other
and are unable to overlook the scars,
the flaws,
blemishes
and each of the things we know you see too clearly.

When we are all looking in the mirror
and seeing different things,
the boldest person we can be
is ourselves.
And even if not one other person could see the girl
for exactly who she is,
she could
she would.

We are searching for loose threads and regrets.
We are searching for anything off centered and weathered.

Today,
she only searched for herself.
The girl who once wished to change too much,
eventually did.

63

The night drips from each of my fingertips,
and I watch it fall onto the center of her chest,
between the inside of each thigh,
and run down the small of her back.

I try and touch her in every place
she has not yet been touched,
I try and get lost in her.
Arch your spine,
grip handfuls of whatever you can,
and speak the filthiest words still living
in the back of your throat.
Your tongue tastes like hell itself,
but it also feels like forever.
So suck out whatever is left of my soul,
and let us see what's inside of me.
What am I made of, really?
I see my own stars in your eyes now,
and they only seem important now that they are there.

If I am a monster,
or made of the most wicked things,
will you still love me?
Perhaps that will be the way we both grow.
If I bring my passion,
will you supply the patience?
Let us undress each other's past,
and shed ourselves of every arrow.

Lay back,

open up for me now.
And when you cannot take anymore,
know that that is what I'm here for.
The same hands reaching through you,
you reach for unknowingly.

I do want to own you,
as you own me,
and make magic that turns the entire world on.

64*

Breaking, then broken
crawling,
standing, then learning
walking, then running......

Remember every time you had to learn
what was left of yourself?
Remember every time you realized
you were not yet finished?
The impossible becomes possible again,
and you show the world once more
your significance.
so you smile,
not because you haven't shed enough tears,
or know the feel of rock bottom,

but you smile
because you survived the very things
you weren't sure you could.

If anything is possible,
maybe everything is possible.
I have to imagine that whatever is next for you
must look a lot like all you've been fighting for.
And if you had to go through it all again,
I can only hope that you would.

This person you are now,
who you've become,
is someone born from the backs of the monsters
we fed
then wed,
and rebuilt with hands
we are only now learning to unfurl.

You are always going to be someone who feels
too much,
who the world assumes is far too resilient to quit
before uncovering the very best of yourself......

and maybe they are right.

65

Love seems to be a timing thing.
I just always seem to be in the wrong places
at the right times,
with a person who feels right
but can't possibly be.

I talk myself into
and out of them.
It's a sickness because I know,
really,
very little of it actually lasts for long.
But this time......
   this time it will be different.
It will count.

I sing myself sweet lies
so I can sleep easily.
Knowing that sometimes the train comes
and goes,

and you are not on it.

Other trains show up, eventually,
and you are free to climb aboard a stowaway.
I'm beginning to think that anyone broken hearted
is only a vagabond
searching for anyone who feels like home.

So when I hear that she gets around,
I cast no judgement.
We are simply laying down with a little wander,
and wonder,
trying not to worry.
Some of us still willing to walk directly on the tracks
as to not miss a train meant for us a second time.
Jump on this one,
hop on that one,
then off at the next stop.

You put your ear to the ground
hoping to hear yours coming,
yet they all start to sound the same.

Maybe you are just a whore like me.
Or,
maybe what we want most
is for the next one
to be the last one.

66

She smelled like sex.
Like sex, and laundry detergent.
Like sex, laundry detergent, and cigarette smoke.
But not her own smoke,
more like she hadn't been alone all that long.
Her unwashed hair hardly reaching her unwashed shoulders,
exposed from a stretched shirt collar.
She wore high wasted denim shorts
and beat up Doc Martins,
and I loved her because she was naked,
raw,
and a very long way from Salt Lake City.

She rummaged around the inside of her bag
for a solid minute,
eventually removing, in a clenched fist,
a yellow lighter and a single Marlboro.
So I was wrong about the smoking thing.
She finished it entirely
in four long, exaggerated drags,
exhaling a jet stream of smoke up,
backwards,
and to the left.

She explained how much she misses mescaline,
and how hard it is to find here.
I told her I had never tried it.

"It's like being in love."
she said.

"Oh yea?" I responded, humoring her,

"You mean like flying too close to the sun?
Or like absolute peace? Like nothing bad even exists anymore?
Like you're finally home?"

"No, because it temporarily makes your heart race,
gives you anxiety,
and normally makes you vomit the first couple of times."

I smiled,
"......and......you enjoy that?"

"I guess I like the idea of it,
more than the thing itself."

67*

You have to be ready to accept some bitterly cold truths.
Perhaps your place in this world
is not as glamorous as you once imagined.
The photo worthy moments
come few and far between,
and we sit so damn long in purgatory
that we become used to the hell of ourselves.

HOPE – that is what they will tell you need more of.
But how long, I wonder,
should you wish for the things extinct?

That is why I say you've just got accept
that some things are not going to go your way,
and that sometimes
the one you fall hardest for
doesn't so much mind the sound
of you hitting the ground.
Relive and kill the thing a million times,
until you are finally able to give life to something,
or someone
else.

Maybe when you are done,
you will be left with more empty frames than photos,
another place you are unable to revisit,

and the first face you see
when walking through the door each day,
is never actually there.

See,
they were wrong…
we all *HOPE* – one way or the other.
Some hope to find their strength again *in* another,
while some hope to find their strength again
without the other.

68*

I swear,
some people just speak so clearly to the parts of us
long since forgotten about.
They find their way in
and it's as if they have been there all along.
Like a part of us belongs to them.

We want answers,
but I am beginning to think there are things
we just aren't meant to know,
no matter how much we tell ourselves we need to.

Maybe everything much less significant
lives wherever it is
that we don't exist?

We're here now,
and I'm not sure what to do
other than continue to fall,
and trust that it will always be safe to uncover
even our ugliest sides.
I am not proud of some of my missteps,
and I know that we are far from perfect,
yet somehow, near you,
I understand that even the imperfect,
the most flawed,
are deserving of their own little corner of the world.

I understand why people say the phrase,
"I can't live without you",
and that even though we both could,
I know for me,
it would mean living a life not worth nearly as much.
I would still chose our corner of the world.
Every day.

After all this time,
I know now,
some people do not just cross your path

they become it.

Don't you see now how foolish
maps
and looking backwards
can be?
Perhaps the answer is to just keep cutting your teeth
on every opportunity,
and learn to embrace
all of the uncertainties.
This may not be your home,
but this space belongs to you
and you alone.

Do you not see your signature on this moment,
how the world is responding,
and that you do indeed
own it?

You are not finished,
you are not yet whole,
and certainly not as you were before.
There is nothing behind you
except lessons from which you have already learned.
There are no plans set in stone,
and the most beautiful thing you have become
is You.
This exact way -
  scar tissue and tears
  and a heart broke wide open
  for the world to hear.

All that is needed is already within
and ahead of you.
Do not avoid anything on the horizon.
Do not walk someone else's path
thinking it safer.

Follow everything that feels right,
let the shadow and shade fall behind,
fall back in love with tonight

and knowing you are enough.

You have always been enough.

70

People say they want to grow with you,
but I doubt they understand what that truly means -
the real weight of it all.

Most people want you ready-made,
only, not made *your* way.
Made *their* way.
In ways that are familiar to them,
that make them feel comfortable,
which fit their sets of standards
and are easy enough for them to stomach.

I like the thinkers,
the square pegs
and the ones misguided.
I like anyone brave enough to change as often
as they feel the need to.

You do not want to grow with people like us.

We will rip both your mind
and goddamn heart out,
purely because we want to see what you're made of.

I find many people are empty inside,
and I love them just the same,

I simply accept that they decided to stop growing long ago,

while we are just getting started.

71*

Dear girl,
tell me your story.
How did you make it this far,
and what is it you are still fighting for?
I see you, and I see someone the world has turned its back on.
And I need you to know how happy I am
to see you standing here.
I see you,
and I see the price some of us pay
simply to live a life.
I see you,
and you become the reason I believe in anything at all,

and I will not give up on you.

I will not quit on you tonight,
and when you do wake
I'll be here still.

Dear girl,
you are not alone.
Sit here, rest with me.
Describe again what hell looks like,
and how you made it out alive.
I see you,
and I realize that the most stunning things
are oftentimes those with imperfections.
I see you,
and I see someone everyone should try and understand.
Someone few ever truly will.

Dear girl,
I want to know you entirely.
Show me who you are becoming,
and I'll show you someone to believe in.

You are everything you ever dreamed of.

72*

Sometimes, the rest of what we leave behind,
is the best of what we leave behind.
And with what remains, we rebuild.
We love harder,
learn to laugh louder,
give more of ourselves to those in need of a hand,
and
albeit slowly, cautiously even,
we go back in search of what defines us.

We believe in things again
eventually,
and though people are unpredictable,
we wrap our arms around them.
The mind will always be a terrible thing to waste,
but the heart is also an awful thing to hide.
There is this little voice, always in the back of our head
telling us that something must go wrong.
Reminding us that nothing good can last forever,
and how all good things
must come to an end.

So we wait……

We wait until we are proven wrong,
or right,
depending on perspective, I guess.
And we wish, deep down,
that people were more comfortable with being vulnerable.
More comfortable with being damaged
so brilliantly
that the world would lift them up for it.
We wish we could see in others
everything we see in ourselves -
the best and the worst.
And that somehow, someway,
we could give so much of ourselves to each other
that there would nothing left to give away.

Sometimes, the rest of what we leave behind
is the best of what we leave behind.

73*

The growth is the work.
A shedding and complete stripping down
of oneself,
shaking free from old beliefs
until we can hardly recognize who
we are becoming.
That is the change they will tell you
you're incapable of.
That is the type of betterment
they wish deep down
you wouldn't buy into.

But they were wrong about you, love.

For some,
the choices become simple:

Growth
or
Death

And once you decide to keep going,
to rid yourself of history and heartbreak,
that decision can be lifesaving.
Not everyone, I know now,
is meant to be along for that transformation.
But transform still.
Evolve.
Fight back against the heaviness of it all.
Dig yourself directly out of everything thrown at you,
piled atop of you,
and never accept the things they try to forcibly label you.

You have come too far to quit now,

too far to stand still in this place.

The growth is the work,
and how simple minded they were for thinking
you wouldn't go work for the best of everything
meant for you,

and still very much alive
inside of you.

74*

Do not believe her to be delicate.
Do not convince yourself
she might be one to take advantage of.
Do not assume her to be weak.

Stare directly into the roughest parts of her,
and try not to look away.
Whether with permission
or not,
even the harshest sides of her
will come to light.

The raw truths of her
brought to the surface.

You should know
she is not for everyone.
She is not made for the masses,
never meant for the senseless
or comfortable in the company of those
who do not challenge her.
If she has learned to live a life fulfilled
on her own,
by all means
enter her world,
but do so only with the intention of enhancing it.

The raw truths of her
will be brought to the surface,
and if you are fortunate enough,
so will yours.

75*

There is something more to you.
Only,
do not expect everyone to see it.
It would be best if you just accepted
that the world will not always recognize
the most important parts of you.
The parts you fought hardest for.

All that I ask
is for you to never hide those parts.
Do not grow so impatient with the world
that you stop being yourself.
Understand that they were not the ones
who had to walk your roads,
who went through all you had to
    to get here.
They were not the ones
who had to learn lessons the hard way,
who were forced to pick themselves back up,
and cut ties
before they were ready to do so.

All that I ask
is that you face this world head on,
and remind it once more

that so much of who you are most proud of,
is made up of those same parts
you fought
and will continue to fight
hardest for.

76*

These things are difficult to explain.
It is still a challenge for me to try and make sense
of us,
how we ended up here,
together,
and why it all seems so worth it now.

So I won't.
Let's not even bother attempting to make sense
of something
which will hopefully always remain larger than either of us
individually.

Instead,
let us simply stay present.
Let us remain in each of these fleeting moments......

holding tightest when we are at our best,
absorbing everything,
every second of it,
feeling it entirely,

and let us learn most
when we are at our worst,
forgiving each other with ease,
yet always growing stronger
because of it.

I suppose there is not going back now anyway.
Sometimes,
heartstrings attach

and even if we could unknot ourselves
from one another,
we would be forever altered.

I have to believe now
that we will never be as powerful apart
as we are together.

It was all worth it.
We were worth it all.

77*

She is an oddity,
a black hearted, blood thirsty angel,
with dirt and Earth beneath her nails.
I like most that she rarely smiles,
but is always laughing in the face of all things ordinary.

Show me your soul,
I'll show you mine,
and with whatever is left of each
maybe we will make something like art.
Something more whimsical than this place,
something more perilous
than what the masses chase after.

Tonight,
tonight can we do something unforgiveable?
If not unforgiveable,
at least something unforgettable.
Tell me how you made it this far
still mostly intact,
slightly obscene
and completely and painfully
unique…

Show me where that dirt came from,
that blood came from,
who it belonged to,

and why those too sweet,
too weak
have absolutely no hope
of surviving you.

78*

There are so many hearts,
so many eyes,
so many laughs,
so many hands out there in the world,

and each of them can affect us
in the greatest and worst of ways.

We have seen and felt quite a few
ourselves,
haven't we?
And yet still, I find myself wanting
to understand yours better.
I find myself wondering what we might be capable of,
wanting to turn over every stone
of who we might become.

I do not simply want us to grow closer
or more familiar
with one another.
That is not enough for me......

When I hear your voice,
I want it to feel like home.
When I feel your touch,
I want it to resonate
so that when you leave me,
I don't feel the full sting of it.
When you smile,
I want to be the reason behind it.

What I'm trying to say
is that I've never known what distance meant
really,
until you were no longer by my side.

And I have never really understood this concept of
everlasting, unconditional

love,

until you were no longer by my side.

79*

There is something to be said
about the ones who have come back
from the brink.
How,
once face to face with the most wicked,
some no longer flinch.
Standing raw, stock-still, exposed,

but unafraid.

There is something to be said
about the pressure necessary
to produce a diamond.
How,
once we are eye with ourselves,
once there are no more lies left to tell,
we're finally unshackled from dreams
that no longer belong to us,
and people
who no longer breathe life
into us.

And there is always something to be said
about those moments wayward,
tormented,
most uncertain.
How the over thinkers can't help but question
the readily accepted,

and how the blackest sheep keep running
from the world's shearing.

There is something to be said,
but the words bring you no justice.
Wounds remain undressed,
scars refusing to fade,
and a spirit pushed past its limit.

But,
don't you know there is no pearl,
where there is no grit?

80*

There is so much life
amidst the things attempting to steal some of our own,
and we can only think to keep beating back at it
with love…

or on some days,
the opposite thereof.

Some days,
the best we can do to be a positive example,
is not nearly good enough.

But I need you to know something…
I need you to hear this clearly –

Even on the days you can barely breathe,
even when every one of your muscles
seem to atrophy,
even when the weight and responsibility
is more than your back can bear…
there is not one single thing behind you,
nor one single thing ahead of you,
that is stronger than who you have grown into.

You are undaunted
even when most shaken,
and perhaps your greatest strength of all
has been learning how to simply continue on,
continue climbing, clawing, crawling through
everything that stands in your way.

So, rough girl,
be gentle.
Weary girl, rest.
Be strong enough to drop your guard,
and let down that wall.
All that lives and breathes behind it
must be starved for something more.

After all this time,
after burning through it all and finally falling,
you have to know that you are right where
you are meant to be.
Exactly where you are meant to be –

stronger in ways,
and smarter in others

ABOUT THE AUTHOR

Father.
Observer.
Thinker.
Writer.

"This country is being managed to death,
being public related to death."
~ Kurt Vonnegut

Let Her Run

39159660R00071

Made in the USA
Middletown, DE
06 January 2017